FUIMOS A CUBA

WE WENT TO CUBA

Yolanda Lopez

BALBOA.PRESS
A DIVISION OF HAY HOUSE

Copyright © 2020 Yolanda Lopez.

All rights reserved. No part of this book may be used or reproduced by any means, graphic, electronic, or mechanical, including photocopying, recording, taping or by any information storage retrieval system without the written permission of the author except in the case of brief quotations embodied in critical articles and reviews.

Balboa Press books may be ordered through booksellers or by contacting:

Balboa Press
A Division of Hay House
1663 Liberty Drive
Bloomington, IN 47403
www.balboapress.com
844-682-1282

Because of the dynamic nature of the Internet, any web addresses or links contained in this book may have changed since publication and may no longer be valid. The views expressed in this work are solely those of the author and do not necessarily reflect the views of the publisher, and the publisher hereby disclaims any responsibility for them.

Print information available on the last page.

ISBN: 978-1-9822-5586-2 (sc)
ISBN: 978-1-9822-5588-6 (hc)
ISBN: 978-1-9822-5587-9 (e)

Library of Congress Control Number: 2020918919

Balboa Press rev. date: 10/28/2020

Also by Yolanda Lopez

Loving Oscar

For Emma, my friend and fellow traveler—
may all our future journeys be filled with the joys
and dangers of that long-ago Cuban holiday.

Travel isn't always pretty. It isn't always comfortable. Sometimes it hurts, it even breaks your heart. But that's okay. The journey changes you; it should change you. It leaves marks on your memory, on your consciousness, on your heart, and on your body.

—Anthony Bourdain

CONTENTS

Illustrations ix

Preface xi

Acknowledgments xiii

Cuba xv

Chapter 1   Havana Bound 1

Chapter 2   Detainment 4

Chapter 3   Eduardo 11

Chapter 4   The Mojitos And More 19

Chapter 5   The Russian Ballet 24

Chapter 6   Playa Maria La Gorda 26

Chapter 7   The Cuban Landscape 31

Chapter 8   The Jazz Café 35

Chapter 9   Cuban Cigars And Rum 39

Chapter 10 Mr. Parakeet 46

Chapter 11 Touring Local Cities 48

Chapter 12 Escaping Eduardo 53

Chapter 13 The Stinky Train Ride 57

Chapter 14 Santiago De Cuba 66

Chapter 15 Baracoa/Guantanamo...74

Chapter 16 Returning To Havana 79

Chapter 17 Too Much Rum.. 84

Chapter 18 Hiding The Cigars 87

Chapter 19 Home At Last... 90

ILLUSTRATIONS

A map of Cuba

The apartment complex (two views)

El Malecon

My Guayasamin painting

Downtown Havana

Playa Maria La Gorda on a cloudy day

Playa Maria La Gorda's palm-tree shelters

Playa Maria La Gorda's red-flag beach closure

A paladore meal in a Havana home

The necklace

The written dedication and program from the Jazz Café

Scenes from the tobacco factory

A Cuban man smoking a large cigar

The rum factory's machines processing sugarcane

Workers bottling rum in the rum factory

Vinales, Cuba

The author in a cave in Vinales

A Cuban bullfinch

The bride and family leaving the church in Trinidad

The train station in Trinidad

The blue toilet in the underground home in Santiago de Cuba

Jaime singing in the bar at the San Carlos Hotel

Jaime in front of the cargo plane

PREFACE

This story recounts a trip my friend Emma and I took to Cuba in the late 1990s. At the time, travel bans prohibited U.S. residents like us from traveling to Cuba. United States' citizens could only enter through Mexico. Cuban citizens were required to return to Cuba through Miami.

As two clueless travelers who really did not know what we were embarking on at the time, Emma and I left San Francisco totally unprepared for the journey that lay ahead. Both of us had traveled extensively, so we were overconfident we could handle any situation. The fact that Emma spoke fluent Spanish added to her and my bravado about traveling to an unknown country that was off-limits to U.S. citizens.

Join me as I share our escapades as we crisscrossed this remarkably beautiful island, from one end to the other, visiting beaches, coastal cities, and a nightclub, all to discover the real Cuba.

ACKNOWLEDGMENTS

I am deeply grateful to my traveling partner, Emma Arroyave, for her continuous encouragement as I wrote our story. She made traveling to Cuba an exciting, joyful event.

I am incredibly thankful for our chance meeting with Jaime, who became an integral part of our trip as we traversed across Cuba. His daring, his courage, his enthusiasm, and his love for the Cuban people are what linger most in my memory. An outstanding traveling companion, he saved us from both small and large disasters along the way.

I am forever appreciative of the wonderful Cuban people we met for their kindness and their unending love of music and country. They generously shared their homes, some unforgettable meals, and their heartfelt feelings. They are what made this a truly memorable trip.

To my initial reviewers, Victoria Chak, and the Pinole Writing Group (PWG), thank you. Victoria, your suggestions were not only insightful but on point. And to my friends in the PWG, I am humbled by your continued support. You laughed in the right places while gently suggesting needed content changes.

Finally, a special thank-you to my daughter, Vanessa Ya Lopez, who served as my technical adviser and who helped design the book cover.

CUBA

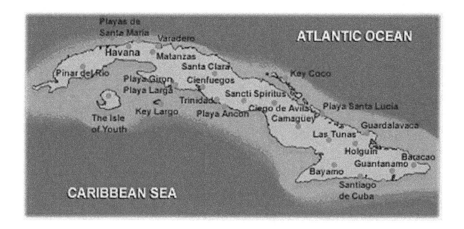

Cuba is 365 kilometers or 226.8 miles south of Miami, Florida. Established on December 10, 1898, Cuba is located in the Caribbean Sea at the entrance of the Mexican Gulf. It is 780 miles long, 119 miles across at its widest points, and 19 miles across at its narrowest points. Havana is its largest city and the capital. Baracoa is its oldest city, founded in 1511. The population of Cuba in 1999, when my friend Emma and I took this journey, was 11.11 million.

Emma and I journeyed across Cuba by bus, train, taxi, and airplane. Our trip took us from the eastern tip of the island, Playa Maria La Gorda, to Baracoa, the westernmost point. Along the way, we visited cities and beaches, including Pinar del Rio, Vinales, Varadero, Cienfuegos, Trinidad, Baconao, Guantanamo, and Santiago de Cuba.

ONE
HAVANA BOUND

Standing back, Emma and I uneasily gazed up at two enormous signs framing the ticket window in the Mexico City airport. One sign said *Belize*, the other *Cuba*. After being temporarily distracted by the bustling travelers all around us who were scattering in different directions, we returned our attention to the ticket counter, hesitating momentarily. Our plan had always been to travel to Belize. It would be simpler, safer. But no, our decision was now made. We would not change it. We drew nearer to purchase our tickets, excited but definitely worried.

Warnings of what could happen if we got into trouble sprang into our heads. It was 1999, and U.S. citizens were banned from entering Cuba. We could face criminal penalties upon re-entry, if caught. But foremost on our minds was our fear of being entirely on our own with no legal recourse or credit cards to rescue us if we needed saving. Surely we were crazy to go so far and risk so much for a mojito.

★★★

It had all begun a few months back, while I was leafing through *Saveur*, my favorite food and travel magazine. The colorful pictures of the celebrated Havana restaurant/bar where Ernest Hemingway had spent time writing and drinking got me imagining what it would be like to see the landmark in person. Restaurante Floridita is famous for several drinks, but it was the pictured rum mojito that tempted me. Shown sitting on a cane table next to outsized chairs with colorful pillows, the drink looked both exotic and alluring in its tall, icy glass with mint floating on top. Soft sunlight filtered through the leaves of live oversize palm trees, giving the restaurant a magical, tropical air. I could almost smell the muddled mint and taste the lingering rum.

The *Saveur* article extolled Havana's growing food and music scene and Restaurante Floridita was at the center of the bustling activity. Photos of the surrounding picturesque, pastel-colored buildings were splashed across the magazine pages. Some buildings appeared to be in advanced stages of deterioration. Many, you could tell, had been elegant queens of a bygone era. It was unclear if the pictured buildings were actually open for business, yet people could be seen entering and departing several, despite their ramshackle appearances.

American cars from the late 1940s and the 1950s crowded in front of the structures. Some vehicles appeared to be in pristine condition, featuring worn, polished leather seats and shiny wax jobs; others were rusted and badly in need of paint jobs. No seat belts were visible in the pictures. In another framed scene, both highly polished and dented sedans edged along the historical El Malecon area. The cars from yesteryear created a nostalgic scene of Cuba's downtown streets in earlier times. I wanted to experience Hemingway's hangout, see those burnished automobiles, and sample that mouthwatering mojito. That meant I had to travel to Cuba. But my desire to go to Cuba and the practicality of getting there were two entirely different matters.

I called up my friend Emma, a fellow traveler, and floated the proposal to her. She loved the idea as she reminisced about how much Cuba reminded her of her hometown, Santuario, Colombia. So it was decided we'd go to Cuba.

We would have to take cash, and Emma and I hadn't the faintest idea of how much money we would need for a fourteen-day trip to paradise.

Emma and I needed to do our research and find a place to stay. We secured maps and read up on the island's history while visions of icy drinks teased us, urging us onward. What we did not do was make a detailed plan of what cities and places we wanted to see, except Hemingway's drinking spot. Doing that planning seemed rather unimportant at the time, even though we were planning on entering a country illegally. All kinds of things could happen. And they did.

TWO

DETAINMENT

When we presented our passports at the Mexico City airport, the ticket agent informed us he would not stamp them in the usual manner because U.S. citizens were not allowed to travel to Cuba. After carefully removing two small sheets of white paper from his desk drawer, he stamped the papers and loosely slipped those into our passport books. He cautioned Emma and me not to lose the sheets and said we had to remove the papers before re-entering the States. Suddenly, it dawned on us we might be in over our heads on this trip.

Emma had a close Cuban friend with family connections in Florida and Havana. This friend had offered to arrange housing for our stay in Havana with relations who lived there. She asked only one favor.

"Would you take drugs for the Cubanos prescribed by American doctors?"

"What kinds of drugs?" we asked worriedly.

"Oh, just digitalis and some other drugs," she replied casually. "There is a lot of diabetes, hypertension, and heart disease in Cuba because of the diet and not enough drugs for the people."

Without further thought, we had immediately agreed to take two full backpacks of medications prescribed by Cuban American doctors in Miami and deliver them to doctors in Cuba. We had not paused for even a second to consider the legality of what we were doing. We were simply too focused on getting to Cuba and having our upcoming adventure to worry about delivering the packages or what the packages contained.

We arrived in Havana late on a rainy evening, tired and excited to have reached our desired destination. Our luggage was going down the luggage ramp when airport security staff approached us and pulled both of us out of the visitors' entry line. Frightened, Emma and I did not understand why this was happening.

We were immediately separated, causing our anxiety to skyrocket. The detention officers offered no explanation, nor had they yet discovered the drugs. The medicines remained on our backs in our individual backpacks, which we had been about to place on the luggage ramp when the officers pulled us out of the line. The backpacks stayed on us as we entered separate interrogation rooms.

The questioning began immediately. Emma spoke fluent Spanish, whereas I had a limited understanding of the language. I could understand as long as the vocabulary was basic. Complex sentences and abstract language were far beyond my comprehension level.

I could not imagine what was wrong since security had not yet discovered the drugs. Emma and I were both terrified and perspiring because we could not communicate with each other to come up with a cohesive plan that would explain the sizable quantity of drugs we were carrying. We both knew we were in serious danger.

With no hint about what was going on, I assumed the problem might be Emma's Colombian nationality. She proudly recounted her home country to total strangers whenever we entered a new country and often identified herself as Colombiana when asked her nationality. In earlier travels, Emma had come under suspicion because of her country of origin even though she traveled under an American passport. Colombia's drug history often placed its citizens under suspicion, particularly at airports.

On my end, the questioning focused on where my grandfather was born. Though I answered he was born in Arizona, I had no clue. He had died before I was born. I had never met him. The agents' faces made it clear they did not believe me. Pointing to a map of the United States on the wall behind the interrogation desk, they asked me to indicate exactly where my grandfather on my father's side had been born in Arizona. Nothing made sense. The focus of the questions seemed insufficient grounds for detention, but I was in no position to argue. There was the language barrier as well. I did not fully understand all the questions. Certain Spanish words eluded me, but I knew we were in trouble. I just did not know why.

My heart beat erratically as my mind cycled endlessly through the various warnings people had given us about if something went wrong. Rights Emma and I enjoyed as U.S. citizens vanished in Cuba. We had been warned we would be entirely on our own. We could not contact the American embassy because one did not exist in Cuba. Nor could we ask for any type of U.S. assistance because of the travel ban. We knew no one in Cuba; we had only the name of the contact for our housing in Havana, which we carried on a small slip of paper. It was not a name we could reveal.

How could we get out of the detention area? As my thoughts raced frantically, I decided we would go back to the United States as soon as we were released from custody. I no longer cared about delivering the drugs, having the mojito, or even seeing Cuba. I just wanted to go home! I was totally terrified.

At the time, I was completely unaware Emma was being questioned about me and my background. The officers kept probing her on where my grandfather was born.

Laughing, she said, "How would I know? What does that have to do with anything anyway?"

Finally, Emma lost her patience with the two Cuban detention officers and demanded an explanation. "Why are we being held here? Tell me."

Hesitantly, they replied, "Your friend is Cuban, pretending to be an American, and it is illegal for Cubans to travel to Cuba through Mexico. Cuban nationals can only enter the country through Miami."

Stunned upon hearing this, Emma guffawed loudly, started laughing, and then stopped when she realized the officers were not laughing but glowering angrily. Exasperated, she retorted, "Well, if she's Cuban, then I'm Chinese." The officers scowled at her.

Emma looked around the interrogation room, briefly glancing down at her backpack on the floor, and said, "Are you kidding? Yolanda is traveling on an American passport and doesn't speak Spanish. This is ridiculous. She is no more Cuban than I am. I am not sure where you got that idea. She has an American passport and a California driver's license. What more does she need to prove to you she is an American? Tell me—what?" It was only when she paused to catch her breath that she realized she had been shouting her questions. Pausing, she reminded herself she'd better tone down her rhetoric, as she was in no position to irritate the officers any further than she already had.

The detention officers were not particularly organized or adept at their job. Their questioning appeared to be pretty careless, with little thought of where the questions could or would lead. Emma saw they were fishing for information. She did not understand why. It was equally evident they did not like direct confrontation. Emma was insisting on an answer, staring them down as she waited for a response.

Glancing at each other for a quick moment, the officers appeared to come to some type of unspoken agreement. Finally, the older officer announced they'd release us, but they would not reveal why they had detained us for almost three hours. Surely it couldn't be because one of us looked Cuban and we had entered the country through Mexico, could it?

Emma and I left our interrogation rooms at the same time, afraid to talk to each other or even make eye contact. Hugging our purses and backpacks closely to our bodies, we rushed toward our luggage, which had been cycling through the baggage carousel during our questioning. We mistakenly thought we would not have to go through a security check again since our luggage had been rotating for hours and hours. However, as we neared the luggage ramp to grab our things, a female security officer signaled us to place our backpacks on the security ramp. This set off our internal alarms because we knew she would see what we were carrying in our backpacks. Emma and I both said a silent prayer.

As the backpacks cycled in front of her, the female officer warily said, "You have lots of drugs on you."

I was determined to let Emma speak. She was fluent in Spanish and could perhaps save us. And, in truth, I was way too frightened to say anything.

Emma stopped, bowed her head, looked at the young security officer, and said, "Yes, it is digitalis and other medicines. American doctors in Miami asked us to bring these medications for the Cuban people here. We understand they are really needed. We have been told there is a shortage of these drugs in Cuba. We don't need them." Emma silently lowered her eyes and appeared to study her shoes in an attempt to calm herself. I tried to contain my hysteria.

For a moment, we were not sure what was going to happen. Would the security officer call back the questioning detention officers? She appeared to be thinking about what to do as she considered us. Then suddenly, she said, "Go. Get out of here quickly." Emma and I scuttled away as fast as we could without calling any special attention to ourselves.

After exiting the airport, we realized we were missing one small suitcase. It was 3:30 a.m. It was hot and muggy, and a light rain drizzled down on our heads as we stood outside, looking around. Deciding it was too dangerous to return inside to recoup the bag, we ran toward the sole cab parked in front of the Havana airport. We jumped in and immediately hugged each other tightly, savoring the realization we were safe for the moment.

THREE

EDUARDO

When the detention officers had repeatedly asked us where we were going to be staying, we had told them we did not have the address, which was true. We had missed our scheduled meeting with the family renting us their apartment. And we were supposed to have received the address at this missed meeting.

Emma and I now whispered in hushed tones, trying to determine what to do, unsure whether the driver spoke or understood English. With us still shaken, it did not help that the driver kept insisting we give him the address of where we were going. We didn't know. We had to call the family. Awkwardly, we asked the driver if he could take us to a location where we could make a phone call. Reluctantly and clearly unhappy about the delay, the cabbie took us to a public phone.

We reached our contact, Eduardo, on the first ring, and he gave us the address where the family was waiting for us. Though we quickly relayed the location to the cabdriver, it was apparent he had lost his patience with us. He clearly wanted to get rid of us as soon as possible.

Light rain continually splashed on the windshield as our driver weaved in and out of the shadowy Havana streets. Finally, he entered a small residential street, pulling directly into an open parking spot in front of a tall, indistinct apartment building. It was late, so most apartments were dark. From the taxi window, we could see that one bottom-floor apartment was filled with people. The lights were low, but through the apartment's slightly opened drapes, we could make out people sitting around a table, eating and drinking.

Leaping out of the cab, our driver began yanking our luggage out of the trunk, roughly tossing the bags onto the middle of the sidewalk. After we paid him, the cabdriver sped away.

Looking at the fading cab, Emma gasped. "I left my glasses on the seat in the taxi. I need my glasses." There was nothing we could do. Standing near our luggage and still trembling from our recent airport encounter, we were unsure how to proceed. We noticed the drizzle had stopped. We thought perhaps that was a good sign.

Still hesitant and not sure if we should head to the peopled apartment, we spotted a man jump up from his seat inside, exit the building, and then walk toward us with open arms in a welcoming gesture. He quickly introduced himself as Eduardo and led us into the apartment. Upon entering, we were bombarded with questions from all directions. Several people wanted to know our names, while others wanted to know why we were so late. We explained that we had been detained but were ultimately released. Everyone wanted to know why. We had no idea what the detainment had been about. None of it made sense, and it had definitely left us panic-stricken and wary. We went on to assure the group we had not given the government officers Eduardo's name.

Emma and I added we were exhausted and wanted to get to the apartment. Ignoring our last comment, Eduardo motioned for us to sit down and have something to eat before we left. Completely fatigued but with no other options, we reluctantly joined the others at the table.

Flustered, we pushed the food piled onto our plates from side to side, feigning eating while smiling and attempting to be polite guests. We couldn't eat. We were still in shock. Eventually, the group asked if we had brought the requested drugs. Happily, we handed over the two filled backpacks, glad to be rid of any evidence that could cause us further difficulties even though, in reality, the drugs had not been the reason for our detainment.

Eduardo began explaining the details of our newly rented apartment. It was his home, but he had moved his family out so Emma and I could reside there—for payment, of course. He cautioned us that no one could know we were renting the apartment because a "special permit" was required for rentals.

Emma and I assumed he did not have the permit because of the worried expression that accompanied his repeated admonitions.

Eduardo continued his explicit instructions, saying, "Do not answer the door. If someone rings the bell. If there are telephone calls asking for anyone in the family, say I am out and will call back. Never identify yourselves." Our new landlord went on and on about the power and water shortages that were regular occurrences in Havana. "Keep two buckets filled with water in the bathroom in case the water gets shut off," he instructed. Eduardo droned on. "The electrical power is prone to shut down at any time with no warning, so it is smart to have lots of candles on hand and know exactly where they are." His motto was "always be prepared."

None of this information sounded appealing to two worn-out travelers. Finally, he uttered what we desperately wanted to hear—he would take us to his place after we finished eating. He couldn't keep from bragging that his place was one of the nicest, most up-to-date apartments in Havana.

By the time we got to his car and on the road, dawn was approaching. We drove and drove until finally Eduardo pointed to the right at a large gray concrete high-rise that reminded Emma and me of pictures we had seen of Soviet buildings from the late 1960s. Studying the high-rise, we saw three concrete industrial buildings in total. Apparently, one of them was to be our new home for the next two weeks.

Pulling into the parking area, we crossed our fingers that there would be an elevator. Though the structure was five stories high, we were not surprised to learn there was no elevator. With that hope dashed, we hoped our rental was at least near the ground floor. No such luck—the apartment was on the fifth floor. Glancing up, we saw the stairwells rose up the building's full height on both the right and left sides of its exterior.

Emma and I began lugging our heavy suitcases up the stairs, careful to avoid banging on the railings since it was early morning and people were still sleeping. Eduardo had not offered to help and had rushed onward, so he was now far ahead of us. We strained to catch up with him.

Finally, we arrived at our "luxury apartment." Eduardo's pride was evident as we toured the two-bedroom apartment with its small balcony, tiny kitchen, and bathroom. Modestly furnished, it was far from luxurious by our standards, but we planned to spend limited time in the apartment anyway. It met our requirements; it was clean and neat, and that was all we really needed.

Eduardo again counseled us about answering the door and the phone and then, as an afterthought, mentioned he kept a parakeet outside on the balcony in a covered cage. He asked that we feed him, bring him in, and allow him out of the cage only in the apartment. We agreed, peeking under the cover to see our new friend, who was bright yellow and green. He did not look too friendly as he silently observed the new tenants, not even issuing a squawking "hello."

Eduardo looked around and then made himself comfortable on the sofa. He did not seem eager to depart. This should have given Emma and me a clue about the days to come, but we were too depleted to notice. We just wanted him to leave. We were desperate to rest after our long, stressful trip. It was now early morning. Finally, Eduardo left, and we went to bed. Emma had trouble getting to sleep, so I gave her one of my sleeping pills. She tossed and turned, finally dozing off. When I jumped into bed, I fell soundly asleep.

What seemed like only moments after we had bedded down, the doorbell rang once and then again. Alarmed, I peeked through the door keyhole and saw it was Eduardo. It had to still be early morning, I thought. But when I turned back to see the wall clock, it read 10:00 a.m. Not sure what to do, I opened the door and let him in. I thought perhaps he had forgotten to tell us something important. We had arrived so late the previous evening that it would have been easy to overlook some detail.

He entered with a big smile and asked if I had seen the small package of Cuban coffee on the kitchen counter that his family had left as a gift. Eduardo then offered to help make the coffee, claiming Cuban coffee is the best in the world. Cubans do love their coffee. Discombobulated and still half-asleep, I watched as he placed an old-fashioned espresso maker directly on the gas burner, letting the water in the pot heat up and the coffee percolate. This process produced thick, dark, rich coffee.

Eduardo said the only proper way to drink Cuban coffee is with lots and lots of milk and sugar. Preferring my coffee black, I ignored his suggestion and poured the freshly brewed coffee into my chipped espresso cup. Gasping after my first taste, I had to restrain myself from spitting the coffee directly onto him; it was so bitter. Now, I understood his caution. Amused, he watched as I added sugar and then some more to make the coffee palatable to drink. I never became a serious fan of Cuban coffee.

Frantically, I tried to make small talk with Eduardo, as Emma had not slept well and was still sleeping. But there were long silences because my conversational Spanish for chitchatting was absolutely nil and Eduardo spoke no English. Part of the difficulty was I could understand the questions he posed but I did not have a sufficient vocabulary to respond in a meaningful way. We plodded along in this manner—with extended, awkward silences—for a while.

Our host was extremely interested in the plans Emma and I had for the day. After I told him we wanted to walk around and get the lay of the land relative to the downtown area, he immediately offered to drive us around Havana. Then, with casual ease, he mentioned his wife and children were waiting downstairs in his car. Surprised, I was at a loss at how to respond, so I nodded my consent. I kept hoping Emma would get up and help our stilted conversation along, but she slept on. She later told me she could hear us talking but was too weary to get up.

FOUR
THE MOJITOS AND MORE

After Emma rose and dressed, Emma, Eduardo, and I ventured out to the car to join Eduardo's wife and two children. Together, we toured downtown Havana, which was filled with tourists—mostly Europeans and Canadians. Then, we stopped at Restaurante Floridita for our mojitos, which were delicious and even better better than pictured in *Saveur*. The mojitos were the reason for our trip, and we dared not miss them after all we had been through. Feeling generous and pleased we had finally arrived at our planned destination, we bought drinks for the entire family.

Our next stop was the famous waterfront known as El Malecon, where seawater laps gently over the retaining wall from time to time and where striking sunsets wow admirers nightly. On occasion, depending on the weather and tides, the calm laps can quickly morph into heavy gushes, with water splashing over the highway onto passing cars. Pedestrians walking along the promenade may occasionally be surprised with a sudden dousing of cold seawater as well. No water surged over our vehicle that bright, sunny day.

After parking, we began our walking tour, visiting the many art galleries lining the streets of Old Havana. Emma and I both purchased art by Oswaldo Guayasamin, whose style of oil painting is reminiscent of Picasso's early work.

During our stroll in Old Havana, we could hear music filling the air. Rhythmic with heavy drums, Cuban music echoed in the streets from the shops that had their doors opened wide to encourage customers' entry. We could also hear music coming from cars whizzing by. Later that day, we observed people in front of a gas station singing as though they were performing on a formal stage. Awestruck, we glanced around and noticed people dancing in the streets, on their porches, and wherever there was ample space to do so. Some motioned for us to join them. We declined with a smile as we walked on.

Slowly, we were becoming aware of how music fused every aspect of Cubans' daily lives. We continued to be enchanted and astonished by Cubanos' love of music and dance. We saw it displayed over and over as we made our way across the island of Cuba.

As Emma, our retinue, and I continued walking along the narrow streets of downtown Havana, we couldn't help but notice a large crowd gathered ahead of us in our path. As we got closer, we could hear shouting and could see two young women on the ground in a physical altercation. Each was pulling the other's hair while loudly screaming Spanish profanities. A throng of spectators milled around the women, watching them intently. These spectators did not intercede or seem interested in stopping the brawl, which surprised us.

Curious, we asked an older woman at the edge of the crowd what was happening. Shaking her head, she said the two women were both prostitutes and were fighting over a man. The bout was about who he belonged to. She went on to explain that there were many hustlers in downtown Havana looking for outsiders to take a "liking" to them. Latching onto a foreigner who would treat them well was one way that young Cuban women could escape poverty and pull themselves up the socioeconomic ladder. They had few other opportunities, we were told. We moved on, sadly aware women's prospects always seem limited—to a much greater degree in third-world countries than in the United States.

Eventually, when we stopped to grab a bite to eat, Emma and I noticed that Eduardo and his family expected us to pay for their lunch and all the incidentals as we moseyed along. Because Eduardo was driving and giving us the grand tour, we willingly agreed. However, it did strike us as awkward and worrisome, as it appeared our host, who was a stranger, was intent on allowing his new tenants to pay for as much as possible. Or was it just our tired imaginations? We chose to believe our exhaustion was influencing our thoughts.

FIVE

THE RUSSIAN BALLET

Eduardo mentioned that he could get us tickets to a Russian ballet that was visiting Havana. "Do we want tickets?" he asked us.

We shouted an enthusiastic "Yes!"

He bought the tickets; we reimbursed him, thanking him profusely for the opportunity to see a Russian ballet live.

When we presented our tickets the following evening, the ticket agent questioned how we had purchased them. Startled by the query, we did not want to disclose who had bought the tickets in case it would cause trouble for our host.

"Tourists are not allowed to use tickets that are for Cuban citizens," we were sternly informed. "Furthermore," the ticket agent added, "you will not be allowed in the main front doors. Only Cubans can use that entrance with your purchased tickets."

This peeved and perplexed us because Eduardo had failed to give us this important piece of information. In addition, we were informed that if we wanted to attend that evening's performance, we would have to exit the building entirely, re-enter through the back door, and then proceed quietly up five winding flights of stairs to the top balcony, where we could sit unnoticed. We wanted to see the ballet, so we followed the instructions, careful not to be seen.

The ballet was exquisite and well worth the required sneaking in and surreptitious stair climbing. But we remained disappointed that Eduardo had not warned us of these restrictions, and we were now starting to have doubts about him.

He had also offered to buy us any incidentals and groceries we needed, claiming he could get a better price as a Cuban citizen than we could get as tourists. We told him we were interested in having a bottle or two of wine at the apartment to drink before our dinner outings. He graciously picked up a couple of bottles for us. Happy, we paid him only to later discover while wandering in a local grocery store that Eduardo had grossly overcharged us. It was then we decided we needed to distance ourselves from him and his offers. We were renting his apartment, not his services, and his actions were becoming irritating.

SIX

PLAYA MARIA LA GORDA

By day three of our trip, Emma and I were eager to explore the most talked-about beach in the Pinar del Rio region of Cuba. The beach, Maria La Gorda, is on the Corrientes Bay about 188 miles from Havana. In order to visit this beach, we needed Eduardo's car because it was almost two and a half hours away. He recommended that a relative of his take us.

When his relation arrived, he advised us there was a weather warning; it might not be the best beach weather. Not so easily deterred, Emma and I ignored his advice, put on our bathing suits, and got into the car, all the time dismissing the swollen, low-hanging gray clouds in the sky. It began sprinkling on our way. Still, we were hopeful the weather would change by the time we arrived at the beach, since Cuba's rain showers are known to quickly turn to sunshine. In fact, it was pretty common Cuban weather.

The beach was starkly beautiful, with palm-tree shelters set back so you could see water reaching the sand's edge. The palm trees provided shade and were large enough to shelter two or three people from the normally blazing sun. But there was no sun that day. Instead of turning to sunshine, the light rainfall had turned into a heavy downpour. Howling winds followed us as we walked down the beach toward the water. That alone was enough to cause me to turn back, running as fast as I could to shelter beneath the first palm tree I reached. While I was crouching over breathlessly, raindrops splattered on my head and shoulders as they seeped through the water-laden palm leaves. I stood up shivering and wondering what happened to our hoped-for sunny day.

I watched as Emma continued walking toward the water and jumped in despite my repeated calls for her to come back. It was raining too hard to be safe, but with the strong winds and heavy deluge, it seemed unlikely she heard my screams. I watched as she swam farther out. Alarmed, I looked around the beach. There was no one else in sight. I did not know what to do. I could not swim, and I would not dare go out there anyway. The shrieking winds and pounding rain made the beach fearsome, especially for a nonswimmer.

I began praying for Emma. It was then I saw a small figure walking in our direction from way down the other end of the beach. I could see it was a man, and he seemed to be carrying two large red flags, but he was too far away for me to see him clearly. He seemed to be having great difficulty holding on to the flags because of the rain and heavy winds. The squalls kept whipping the flags in different directions, but he held on to them tightly.

He abruptly stopped near where Emma had entered the water. I could see he was shouting something out toward the water but could not make out what he was saying. I was sure Emma could not hear nor see him. She was too far out at that point. The torrential rain continued. He placed one of the large red flags over the other one and held them both up high over his head. We did not know its meaning at the time, but later learned this meant the beach was closed for public use. Emma continued swimming.

The man then started jumping up and down in a pantomime fashion, signaling her to get out of the water. Finally, Emma saw that something was going on at the shore, but even then, she did not think it was about her. Trudging out of the water, she slowly made her way toward the man. I could see he was agitated. When she reached him, he started speaking loudly and pointing toward the water. I was so happy she was out of the water that I started running toward them. He explained excitedly that there had been deadly poisonous jellyfish swimming all around her in the water.

He could see them from the shore. "One bite," he told us, "could be fatal." He said the high winds and currents had disturbed them, bringing them to the surface. Emma said she had seen the masses all around her but thought they were seaweed.

He shook his head and said, "You were lucky. Why didn't you come in when I signaled you?"

Emma explained she did not see him in the beginning, and when she did, she did not think he was beckoning her. He batted his head in clear frustration and said the beach was now closed. "Did you see anyone else in the water?"

"No," Emma replied. "I was concentrating on swimming and enjoying myself."

Picking up his drenched flags, the man turned around without another word and headed back the way he had come. With Emma "safe on dry land," we agreed it was probably not the best day for the beach, after all.

The rain continued falling steadily. Soaked and relieved that Emma had not had any jellyfish mishaps requiring medical treatment, we packed up and headed to the car of our driver, who merely shook his head as we got into the vehicle. Emma and I had made a commitment to each other that we would not enter a Cuban medical facility under any circumstances. We had been warned and were heeding that caution.

SEVEN
THE CUBAN LANDSCAPE

The next day, we decided to stick closer to home. To our dismay, our host continued showing up each morning. We had no idea how to discourage him. So, Emma and I decided we needed to get away from the apartment and Eduardo. We politely declined his services, saying we wanted to walk around on our own. He left disappointed. We were relieved to be free from his constant petitions to assist us.

We headed out the door toward the water. As we strolled along the water, we passed a tall, young stranger whom we took for an American. We'd not seen a single fellow American so far, and we were overjoyed to meet one. However, when he greeted us with a "hello," we knew he was Canadian by his accent. He extended both hands toward us, and it was then we noticed he was holding two rolls of toilet paper. He asked if we needed toilet paper, explaining there was a serious shortage in Cuba. Later, we learned that toilet paper would disappear from hotel rooms once guests left for a meal or a day's outing. Hotel staff stole it, along with any remaining soap. Surprised by his unusual but generous offer, we declined. We had been told by the Miami Cubans to bring candy, pencils, and our own toilet paper, so we were adequately prepared.

Everywhere we walked, Cubans approached us, soliciting us for money, often relaying sad stories of not being able to feed their children. They would tug at our sleeves and our heartstrings to get our attention as they followed us. Some were more desperate than others. We had been advised not to give out money because it would encourage large crowds, it could get dangerous, and it could get us in trouble. Emma was kindhearted and often got into extended conversations with the people following us. Frequently, she ended up giving them money. I kept reminding her to watch her dwindling funds because we could not get any more while in Cuba. Eventually, she did run out. Luckily, I came to Cuba with adequate funds and could share them with her.

The limited availability of food for Cuban citizens disturbed us. Cubans ate lots and lots of fried chicken and white rice. Fried chicken seemed to be a Cuban staple; it was the meal most often served to us whenever we ate out. Emma hated fried foods. She particularly disliked a strange-looking type of pork we were served on several occasions. Normally, there were no vegetables, fish, or salad on the menu. The scarcity of fish for citizens confused us since Cuba is an island surrounded by water, so surely, there was plenty of fish for everyone. We were told that not only was fish expensive, but its purchase was limited to Cubans but not tourists.

Besides making constant requests for money, hangers-on offered their homes as places to eat. Many Cubans served meals in their homes to boost their incomes. These places were called *paladores*. We ate in many of them. They served excellent food, never fried chicken or white rice. We had some astounding paladore meals we will never forget. I still remember the aroma of one meal, a fabulous fish dish, sizzling in a pan. The host's presentation of the delectable treat required that I take a picture of it in order to preserve it in my memory.

In addition to the people following us, a lengthy line of scraggly dogs trailed us. Emma was heartbroken at how emaciated the animals looked, malnourished with skimpy fur and clearly visible ribs. She began dispersing small bits of food she had not eaten on the ground behind her as we sauntered along. Tourists and citizens stared at us as we walked along streets with a line of Cubans and dogs trailing behind us.

EIGHT
THE JAZZ CAFÉ

As we ambled down one of Havana's main streets, a Cuban woman in her late sixties began tugging on our sleeves. Her request was so significantly different from the others that we stopped and listened. With our full attention, she said that she wanted to invite us to her jazz club, where she was the star performer. She wanted us to hear her sing that night. And she promised if we came to her performance, she would dedicate a special song to us. As she spoke, we stared doubtfully at her, but we indicated that we would try to come. After that, the woman disappeared from the trail of dogs and people behind us.

Emma and I debated whether there was really a club and if she actually was the featured singer as she had proclaimed. Emma thought we should go.

Later that night, we made our way to the address the songstress had given us. Upon arriving, we were both surprised to find an actual nightclub called the Jazz Café. After paying at the door, we rushed in and found seats at a table near center stage. Shortly thereafter, club staff approached us and told us we had not paid to enter. Agitated and still unsure why we had come, we patiently explained that we had paid the two guys standing at the door. Apparently, the original collectors were street people, not café staff. Even though we made a fuss, insisting we had already paid, we went with the staff back outside the club and each doled out two additional pesos to keep our seats. Staff then issued us a strong warning to not pay anybody standing at the door as we turned to re-enter the club. How could we have possibly known who was and wasn't staff?

Upon returning, we discovered several men had made themselves at home at our table. Sitting down, we asked them to leave. Instead, they commenced making flirtatious comments. When we signaled we had no interest in their company, they started bombarding us with insults, saying that we were most likely gay and only loved women, not real men like them. That was the only possible reason we would not welcome their company. Laughing at this reasoning, we focused on our drinks and ignored the men. Frustrated, they finally got up and left. Rattled and rethinking our visit, we pondered whether it had been a good idea to show up at the jazz club, with its double entrance fees and hassling patrons.

Shortly thereafter, the lights dimmed, and the music started. To our utter wonderment, the spotlight shone down on the very woman who had followed us. She came out dancing and singing. Flabbergasted, we found it hard to believe it was the same woman. Looking fabulous and like the star she was, Monica, the jazz singer, not only sang but was a graceful dancer.

After a couple of introductory songs, she made her way to our table and welcomed us. As the spotlight flashed down on Monica, Emma noticed her necklace, which was made up of individual stones, each picturing a different saint. Emma ogled it, exclaiming how lovely it was. Monica immediately bent down, removed it from her neck, and handed it to her. Emma tried to refuse, but Monica was insistent, so Emma happily accepted the gift.

Then Monica sang a special song dedicated to us as her special guests. The music and dancing were remarkable. Everyone was dancing. Despite the fuss about getting into the venue, we were now thrilled we'd come.

As the evening drew to a close, the Jazz Café star, Monica, signed our programs with an affectionate dedication that read, "Remember this night in Cuba with Monica and Vincente, with much love (November 13, 1999)."

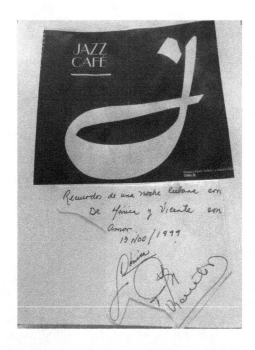

NINE

CUBAN CIGARS AND RUM

Despite the hot, humid weather, Emma and I were eager to tour the local cigar and rum factories. During our trip, we'd seen women, particularly older Cuban women, smoking extra-long, fat cigars. We'd seen men smoking them too. The cigars looked nothing like the ones we were familiar with from the States. Thicker and so much longer, they had a milder aroma than those back home. They were bulky, dark brown, and not particularly attractive when compared to ones we were familiar with. Later, we saw beautiful premium Cuban cigars that were costly and attractive.

Everyone seemed to smoke, with the younger women favoring the smaller, thinner cigars or cigarettes and the older Cuban women seeming content with the big, fat cigars. Neither Emma nor I smoked, but the Cubans we met kept encouraging us to try smoking. Cuban products were different from the American ones, we were told. The tobacco was milder and sweeter. Curious yet well aware of the perils of smoking, we decided to try cigarettes. We enjoyed them immensely; they were truly better tasting than the American ones. Even so, neither of us ever smoked cigarettes again. But we bought plenty of the big, fat cigars for gifts.

Cuba is famous for its superior cigars, which are smoked worldwide. And Havana in particular is known for premium cigars. The city is dotted with cigar factories of all sizes. Although the most famous one is the Partagas Cigar Factory, we elected to tour an old-world one. We were overwhelmed by the grassy scent of fresh tobacco leaves that pressed upon us as we entered the poorly lit and shoddily constructed building. A large room held rows and rows of workers seated side by side and engaged in different aspects of the cigar-making process. The seating arrangement resembled that of a grammar school.

In addition to the grassy scent, a strong ammonia odor permeated the air. When we asked the guide about it, he said the weight of the stacked tobacco leaves generated heat, up to 100 degrees Fahrenheit, and that heat caused the expulsion of ammonia and other unpalatable organic compounds.

Not only was the factory crowded with workers, but it had tobacco paraphernalia strewn about on two large tables that ran along the sides of the room. Besides the equipment, the corner held stacks of piled high tobacco leaves.

Our guide pointed to workers using thimble knives fitted to their fingers. Those special knives allowed them to remove the main vein of the filler leaves—delicate work that had to be done by hand. Removing the vein ensured the cigars would burn evenly. Afterward, workers stacked the stripped tobacco leaves into piles to be used later for rolling and wrapping cigars.

We learned about all aspects of tobacco harvesting, beginning with how tobacco leaves are cured to develop their unique aroma and appearance. The leaves, the guide told us, are hung from the ceiling in a curing barn, where they slowly change color from dark green to brownish yellow. Workers then sort the leaves by color and size; the smaller ones and the broken ones are set aside for cigar filler while the larger leaves are used for inner wrappers or binders. Tied into bundles of ten to fifteen leaves, the cigars are then placed in casks, where they are aged from three months to five years.

At this point, the leaves undergo a chemical change called *fermentation*, which develops the leaves' aroma and taste. Even once fermentation has occurred, micro-fermentation will still occur in the tobacco, which will rid the tobacco of some by-products of fermentation. By-products such as ammonia and other compounds can make the tobacco's flavor acrid and unpleasant unless dissipated.

This entire fermentation process, which determines the tobacco's flavor, relies on tradition, taste, and legacy. It depends on the individual factory's history and the cigar master's decision on how long to allow fermentation. According to our guide, this is where the true art of cigar making really begins.

The last step is aging. Again, longtime practices play a role in determining how long to age cigars, since aging establishes the final flavor. Over time, the flavors mellow and blend, resulting in a smoother taste and fewer off flavors. Thus, longer-aged cigars will often be mellower due to the reduction of chemical by-products. Aging is the secret to creating the finest cigars.

As we wandered around and listened, we passed workers who discreetly extended their hands out, palm up, requesting money. They kept their hands low, so the floor supervisor did not see. The workers were insistent and strongly shook their palms to make their point when we failed to place coins or paper money in them. Frankly, their demanding requests caught us off guard. We gave them the few coins and pencils we had on us. They did not seem especially pleased with Emma and me. Most likely, management knew what was going on and chose to ignore it.

Later, after returning to the apartment, Emma and I struggled to smoke one of the purchased cigars. Lighting it proved to be a challenge, but we finally got it lit and attempted to smoke it. After several bouts of sputtering, coughing, and failing to keep the cigar continually lit, we gave up in total frustration. This meant we were taking more cigars home, although we knew we might have trouble sneaking them through customs upon our re-entry to the United States.

The fascinating cigar factory tour had taught us a lot about tobacco and cigars. The rum tour was next. Emma and I could hardly wait. We loved rum. We were planning on enjoying this tour tremendously because we had heard you are allowed to try as many samples as wanted.

Sugarcane sweetness wafted through the air as the guide led us into an old ramshackle building covered with cane and bamboo leaves. It was very primitive by any modern standards. As we neared the entrance, we saw employees brandishing machetes and cutting the sugarcane in the boiling sun. Our tour guide explained how the raw sugarcane is cut, and he allowed us to sample the sugarcane before it was processed.

The tour guide stated that Cuba's fertile soil and tropical climate produce the finest sugarcane. Cuban sugarcane has low viscosity, is low in acidity, and is high in sugar, all of which make it ideal for distilling. He added that the Cuban method of distilling is often imitated, but without the Cuban sugarcane, it will not produce the same rum.

Cuban rum is double distilled. This two-step process starts with creating vino de cana (fermented molasses), which is distilled at 75 degrees Celsius in a copper-lined column still to get aguardiente (an anise-flavored liqueur made from distilled sugarcane). Then, this is charcoal filtered, aged for two years, blended with a sugarcane spirit, and distilled in a multicolumn still. This process is what gives Cuban rum its light character.

We then toured the bottling and labeling area. Excited about the quality and quantity of the rum, especially after tasting all the samples, we bought four bottles of the best Cuban rum, two for Emma and two for me. We wanted to take them home but were not sure we could pull that off. We plotted how we would get our yummy rum home. If we couldn't, we would have to drink the bottles before leaving for home.

Again, the workers overwhelmed us with requests for money. We had no coins left, so we were unable to give them any.

TEN

MR. PARAKEET

While lugging our rum up the stairs to the apartment, Emma and I thought we should check on our charge, Mr. Parakeet. Worried that he probably needed to be fed, we clumsily rushed to feed him while his cage remained on the balcony.

As we opened the latch, Mr. Parakeet flew skyward, escaping to the huge trees surrounding the large complex. Panicked, we ran down the four flights as fast as our tired legs could go, trying to keep him in sight. Gasping as we reached the bottom steps, we scanned the sky and nearby trees for any sign of him. Failing to see any trace of him or even hear his irritating squawks, we debated what to do or what to say to the family about the now-missing bird.

We thought we could perhaps buy another bird that looked like the missing one, put it in the cage, and pretend it was the same bird. For a moment, we gave this serious consideration. Then, we remembered we hadn't really bothered to study Mr. Parakeet all that closely, so we weren't even sure we could find a close match that would fool the family. Troubled and resigned, we trotted back upstairs, called Eduardo, and confessed. Mr. Parakeet's owner said he would be right over to help us find the missing bird, which he stressed was a "valued" family member.

Eduardo arrived quickly, equipped with a large net attached to a long-handled pole. He asked us to retrieve the cage from the upstairs balcony. While we were racing back up the stairs, he began searching the trees. After lugging the cage down the steps, we caught up with Eduardo and then straggled close behind, annoyed with ourselves for our stupidity. Somehow, Eduardo located Mr. Parakeet in a nearby tree and managed to lure him back into his cage. Perhaps the bird's break for freedom was not a one-time incident since his recapture seemed suspiciously practiced.

Emma and I were overjoyed and oh so relieved, and we thanked Eduardo profusely. We resolved to never open the cage's latch again while the cage sat on the balcony. As soon as Eduardo left, we turned around and made a face at Mr. Parakeet. He stared back at us with what appeared to be a fully satisfied look that said, "Hey, I escaped for a short while."

ELEVEN

TOURING LOCAL CITIES

Cuban Bullfinch (Melopyrrha nigra)
© 2010 Photo by Rajoch
http://en.wikipedia.org/wiki/File:Melopyrrha_nigra.jpg
Licensed under Creative Commons
Attribution 2.0 or later version

Emma and I wanted to visit cities near Havana before trekking across the island. Hearing rumors of astounding caves in **Vinales**, a city 115 miles southwest of Havana in Pinar del Rio Province, we headed there. Founded in 1878, Vinales remained a sleepy agricultural village surrounded by the Sierra de los Organos, a low-lying mountain range. The western part of town was designated as a national park (Valle de Vinales National Park) and is home to dozens of exotic bird species, including the Cuban bullfinch, a songbird variety of the genus *Melopyrrha* that is found mainly in Cuba.

As we neared the village, a noticeably pungent smell drifted our way, making our noses twitch. We soon learned it emanated from the lush, green tobacco plants we could see swaying in the fields all around the town. Vinales farmers grew tobacco for cigars but did not handle any part of the actual cigar-production process. Instead, they sent their dried tobacco to the larger towns and cities for hand rolling and finishing.

Our focus was on seeing the caves. There were lots of choices, so we decided to visit several. When we entered our first cave, stifling heat overpowered us. It made us sticky and uncomfortable. Then, we noticed a strong, musty smell. Most likely, it was from mold and the guano (bat excrement) that covered the cave walls. Though the cave was mostly dark, certain sections were more visible as beams of daylight filtered through cracks. In those sections, we could just make out the high curvature of the walls, which gave us a fuller grasp of the cave's depth. We exited breathless and speechless at the grandeur of our first cave.

The second cave we entered was artificially lit so visitors could get more impressive views of the deeper inlets. This also gave us a greater appreciation for the size and expansiveness of the cave's interior. We marveled at the beauty of the cave.

In the end, we did not have time to see the cave that offered a boat trip along part of the subterranean river that runs under the mountains, where we could have seen stalagmites and stalactites. Returning to town, we wanted to explore Vinales's main street, which is lined with colorful wooden houses.

Emma and I also wanted to explore the coastal cities, so we went to **Varadero**, a resort town in Matanzas Province located along the Atlantic Ocean coast. Founded in 1887, this city began as a small summer resort. No longer small during our visit, it had some hotels. Today, however, rows and rows of exclusive hotels dot the Atlantic coastline.

Varadero is home to the Reserva Ecologica Varahicacos, situated near the eastern tip of the city. This preserve features trains and ancient burial caves. Also, there is a famous park (Parque Josone), which opened in 1942. It is filled with lovely ponds and gardens. Though Varadero had more caves to explore, we elected to skip them, having done our cave exploring in Vinales. After short visits to the reserve and Parque Josone, we donned our bathing suits and walked to the beach for a day of sunning—our goal while traveling along the Cuban coast.

Having heard of the splendor of **Cienfuegos**, a city on Cuba's southwest coast, we scheduled it next. Located 160 miles from Havana and dubbed La Perla del Sur (the Pearl of the South), the city was named after Jose Cienfuegos, a man who was part of an early French settlement in 1829. Many street names in Old Town (an older section of the city) still reflect the city's French origins.

The central square features a park called Parque Jose Marti. Within the park resides the Thomas Terry Theatre. Beautiful gold-leaf mosaics cover the lower walls of this building, and the ceiling showcases stunning frescoes. After spending ample time admiring the theater, we hiked over to the Jardin de Cienfuegos, located east of the city. This garden features hundreds of native tropical plants. From there, we took a quick detour to visit the Catedral de la Purisima Concepcion, which originally opened in 1833 and was declared a cathedral in 1903. Entering the church, we kneeled on the plain wooden pews and prayed for a safe trip as we continued moving through Cuba.

We returned to Havana slightly sunburned but refreshed by our visit to the coast.

The doorbell rang at nine o'clock the next morning, the fourth day into our trip. We knew who it was. We had a problem. Hesitantly, I opened the door to see Eduardo's smiling face. He asked me if the coffee was ready and what were our plans for the day. Again, he offered to be our driver. We told him we were going to do some shopping and we were thinking of taking a one-day overnight trip to Trinidad, a beautiful city located in central Cuba, about two hundred miles from Havana, that has old churches and a tropical jungle atmosphere. It was once the center of the sugar-trade industry, and it has the reputation of being the best-preserved Spanish colonial town in Cuba.

Eduardo left shortly after drinking his coffee, and we could sense his acute disappointment. We knew we had to escape his constant attention again. It had gotten claustrophobic.

As soon as he left, we went out and bought tickets to Trinidad for the following day. We packed for a one-day stay. We excitedly looked forward to exploring some voodoo venues in Trinidad we had heard about, though we knew well enough not to mention this to Eduardo. We had heard there might be some practitioners there.

With arrangements for our trip settled, we let Eduardo know we would be away for a one-day trip.

TWELVE

ESCAPING EDUARDO

Stepping onto our bus to **Trinidad** the next day, Emma and I breathed a sigh of relief. We were once again on our own without someone hovering over us.

The bus dropped us off in the main plaza, where a wedding ceremony had just ended. The bride and groom were standing in front of the church, posing for pictures, laughing, and smiling at the curious tourists who were wishing them well as they passed. We could faintly hear music playing in different sections of the plaza. We had arranged to spend the night in a local hotel and relished being in a much smaller city than Havana.

Yolanda Lopez

At nine o'clock the next morning, we were thrilled there was no smiling host ringing our bell or asking us for coffee. Emma and I dropped into the hotel's restaurant for breakfast and were deep in conversation when an unknown man appeared next to our table. Pointing his index finger at me, he unabashedly began talking quickly. I was not sure what he was saying to me, but I latched onto a word I did understand: *sex*. He kept repeating it over and over. I glanced at Emma, who appeared to be angry and agitated.

"What is he saying?" I asked. "Emma, tell me. What is he saying?" Though I asked her repeatedly, she remained silent for a couple of minutes.

Finally, she said, "He wants you to go to his room now. He is asking how much you cost."

Stammering, I asked, "What is this about?"

Emma shook her head and talked louder and louder by the minute in response to the stranger's insistence I leave with him. Later, she would tell me the man explained he was a famous Spanish matador, everyone knew him, and he wanted me to go with him and refused to take no for an answer. I was frustrated because I did not understand most of the conversation between Emma and the matador. I could see Emma was flustered and incensed. Meanwhile, the bullheaded matador was not budging. Eventually, my friend said something that caused the matador to stomp off.

We later learned that Cuban women do not go to public restaurants to eat as we had done and that he probably assumed we were prostitutes. This made us laugh since we were hardly dressed the part. We looked shabby and ragged in our American clothes. We had no nice clothes with us, nor did we even remotely resemble the young, beautiful, well-dressed prostitutes we had seen on the Havana streets.

I regretted not knowing more Spanish words for sexual encounters so I could have understood exactly what the man said he wanted me to do for him. Emma refused to tell me what his request was and what she had said to get him to leave. Simply shaking her head, she kept her lips sealed on both matters.

After our encounter in the restaurant, we wandered around the city, visiting local churches. We had no luck in locating any voodoo shops or practitioners, so we returned to the central plaza. Vendors had set up stalls all along the perimeter and were marketing their handmade items. Emma and I meandered around the square, buying handmade lace, and making sure to keep track of the time, as the bus returning to Havana was scheduled to leave at 3:00 p.m.

The bus pulled up right on time, and passengers started scrambling onto it. Emma and I looked at each other and said, "What if we don't get on it?" We had only moments to decide. In the blink of an eye, we chose not to get on, and we watched the bus drive off without us. It was a spur-of-the-moment decision made without much thought as to what would come next. We had brought clothes for one day. Our goal had merely been to extricate ourselves from Eduardo. We looked around and consoled each other, saying, "It's all right. We could travel to another city by bus."

THIRTEEN

THE STINKY TRAIN RIDE

As the bus rolled away, it dawned on us we needed a plan before it turned dark. "Well, let's just go to the next city. How hard could it be? We got to Trinidad relatively easily," we said animatedly, not really having any idea how far away the next city actually was. We had not brought along any of our maps.

We soon found out, to our dismay, that the only way to get to the next-largest city was by train. No buses traveled there. We had been warned repeatedly to never travel on Cuban trains. They were dangerous and dirty, and pickpockets roamed everywhere, or so we had heard. Looking solemnly into each other's eyes, Emma and I silently agreed to risk it. We asked a passerby where we could buy train tickets. He pointed to a building across the plaza.

Confidently, we ambled over to the large yellow building, where indoor and outdoor seating was available. Groups of people sat or milled about inside and outside the edifice. We wandered inside, mistakenly believing this was where to buy train tickets. We quickly learned this was only the building where groups assembled to go to the train station. Here, people got transported by cab to the actual train station, where tickets could be purchased.

The agent in this building informed Emma and me that we had an insufficient number of people in our group; two people were not enough. This made no sense to us—what difference did two or four people make if we were taking a cab?

Glancing around, we noted most people seemed to be in large family groupings. How were we going to cobble together a bigger group to proceed to the train station? It was still light outside, but dusk was looming. Confused, we returned to the agent and asked

Fuimos A Cuba

for a recommendation. Pointing to a man sitting in the corner with a bike, he said, "Check with him. Maybe he will join your group. He is alone."

Shyly and slowly, we approached the man and asked if he would join us to reach the required group size. Smiling broadly at us, he said his name was Jaime, he was a Spaniard, and he would be happy to be part of our group. He asked if we were traveling alone, noting it was very unusual for Americans, particularly women, to be traveling in Cuba. We nodded. We noticed he had a cell phone, something we'd not yet seen in our travels in Cuba, which really caught our attention.

He asked where we were going, and we said to Santiago de Cuba. "Do you have a place to stay?" he inquired.

Sheepishly, we explained we had no particular plans or place to stay; we were on a last-minute journey. We didn't want to explain we were running away from Eduardo. Still grinning, he said, "Good, then join me. I know the underground system here."

We did not know what the underground system was, but we smiled in agreement. Jaime then explained he had been traveling with a German friend who met up with a woman in Havana and then decided he did not want to leave her or continue on his and Jaime's planned trip.

"She's probably a prostitute. I tried to warn him, but he wouldn't listen, so I left without him. We were supposed to cycle across Cuba. He deserted me and abandoned our bike trip. I'll go across Cuba with you and then on to South America as planned."

It was only then that we noticed his unusual bike—small, silver—which appeared to be foldable. Emma and I had never seen anything like it. Seeing us staring at it, he said that it was awfully expensive and that he never let it out of his sight. He referred to his bike as "mi esposa" (my wife). We thought it odd, but lacking any appropriate response, we remained silent, gazing at him and his bike. He went on to tell us he came to Cuba often and knew it well. This time, he had come to bike across the country, but that trip, as he said, had failed. The fact that he had firsthand knowledge of Cuba and a cell phone was all the encouragement we needed to partner with him.

Jaime was handsome with a full head of wavy, jet-black hair and an outgoing personality. Although Emma and I had only been looking for additional bodies to board the train, we had stumbled upon so much more. It seemed we had accidentally found a knowledgeable traveling companion. Somehow, we decided to trust him, even if all we knew was what he chose to reveal. Whether it was true, we had yet to know. As it turned out, Jaime proved himself the perfect companion for crisscrossing Cuba.

We quickly learned Jaime was fun, flirtatious (not with us), and an excellent singer. But, more important, he was extremely resourceful and able to get us out of sticky situations when needed. Jaime, in turn, was amused by our total lack of direction, our ignorance about where we were going and how we were getting there. Despite that, Jaime must have deemed us acceptable as travel companions. He and Emma remained friends long after our trip, corresponding for a period of years.

Returning to the agent, we declared we now had our group. The agent advised us to wait; he would call us when it was time to go. In the meantime, Jaime explained to us that there were two monetary systems in Cuba, one for the locals and one for the tourists. We were going to be locals, he told us. Since he and Emma were both fluent in Spanish and I wasn't, he asked that I remain silent whenever we were negotiating or buying anything and particularly when we got into cabs.

While we were waiting, the sky darkened to an indigo blue. I got nervous, recalling all the admonitions we had been given about trains. Emma and I really had no clue what we were doing, where we were going, or how we were going to stay safe on the train. And we were traveling with a man we had randomly met at the station.

When I expressed my train fears out loud, Jaime laughed and reassured me, saying, "Trains aren't that bad. Yes, they are smelly, and you must be careful. But it is ok to use them."

Easy for him to say, I thought. Although unconvinced, I managed to keep quiet.

After the agent signaled us to move forward, I pushed down my anxiety as we climbed into a cab and sped off to the train station. It was now late evening and pitch-black. As the taxi came to a halt, I was troubled by what I saw. The train station's silhouette appeared in the foreground as that of a large rectangular warehouse. It was completely dark. We paid the driver and shuffled along with our suitcases toward the edifice.

Upon entering the station, we were told there was a power outage, so there were no lights. We could see people's shadows, but we couldn't make out distinct faces, just the silhouettes of bodies huddled together in a lengthy line. Scary as it was, I reluctantly got in line. Emma and Jaime did not seem too disturbed by the sight. One small votive candle glowed at the ticket window. It was the only illumination in the entire building other than the edges of burning cigarettes. All the warnings Emma and I had received sprang into my mind, frightening me further. The only saving grace was that we had Jaime with us, and he was an imposing figure, standing over six feet tall.

We were advised to have our money out and ready before reaching the ticket window. At this, I discovered I only had hundred-dollar bills left in my wallet. Emma and I had brought lots of cash into Cuba because we couldn't use credit cards. I had brought four thousand U.S. dollars in hundred-dollar bills so it would not be so bulky and obvious and so we did not run out of money. I worried and hoped the ticket agent would accept a hundred-dollar bill.

When I put my money down on the counter, the ticket agent threw the hundred back at me and said, "Are you crazy? We don't make change for that kind of American money." Immediately, Jaime came up behind me and paid for my ticket, saying I could pay for him later when I got change. I was so grateful.

With tickets in hand, Jaime, Emma, and I moved to the far side of the building and waited for the train. There were no seats, so we stood in the dark, contemplating what lay ahead. We had bought first-class tickets, thinking the higher fare might favor us with better seating in a safer location.

The train arrived around midnight. Entering the train, we showed our tickets to the conductor. He led us through train car after train car. On and on we went. Foolishly, we thought that first class must be at the end of the train, so we temporarily remained pleased with our decision.

Finally, the conductor signaled us to take some seats. The only problem was there were people sitting in them. Roughly, he told them to clear out. The passengers jumped up, relinquishing their seats but not before giving us dirty looks as they shuffled away. That was how we learned there was no such thing as first class on Cuban trains. To keep my belongings safe, I sat on my suitcase the entire trip.

The train was freezing. I had no jacket or sweater. Emma and I had packed for one night, so we had limited clothing. Determined to warm myself up, I wrapped my pajama top around my shoulders. At the time, I could not understand why the train was kept so cold, but later, I understood the reason for the train's glacial temperature. It was meant to squelch the terrible smell wafting to all corners of the train. An overwhelming stench from the restrooms permeated the air and extended to the far end of the train, where we sat. I vowed to skip using the bathroom until we arrived at our next destination, eight hours down the road. Braver than I, Emma made her way to the restroom, and upon returning, she said it was dirty and gross, but she could not wait eight hours.

The train stopped often. People jumped on and off at each stop. Vendors roamed the aisles, selling food and trinkets at the train stops. Sometimes, the hawkers would display their wares and food near the open train windows, negotiating their transactions before the train moved on. We had brought no food with us but were leery about purchasing food from the vendors, so we bought nothing and watched wistfully as others munched on their snacks. Various food aromas filled the car, making our tummies growl. We ignored the rumblings and concentrated on keeping warm.

To my dismay, there was no bathroom at the end of the line. Public bathrooms were limited in Cuba at that time. Restrooms were usually just in private homes and in a small number of restaurants. They were hard to find. If you were fortunate enough to locate one, you had better have brought your own toilet paper, as there was unlikely to be any. Sometimes but not always, vendors stood guard by the door, selling one or two single sheets for coins.

By the time we arrived, I was in desperate need of a bathroom. But because we could find none, Jaime said I would have to wait until we got to our new rental. I mustered every ounce of strength left in me to keep from crying out loud, knowing it might not be possible to delay "nature's call" any longer after the all-night train ride.

Jaime had spent his time on the train trying to arrange for underground housing prior to our arrival. Fortunately, he was able to secure a place in a private home. We left the train station and made our way there.

Our first underground housing location was a pleasant, small home. Upon entering, I immediately asked for the bathroom, explaining my urgent need. The lady of the house kindly led me to the restroom. Rushing in, I breathed a sigh of relief. My crisis had been averted. Emma and I shared a room, which was clean and restful. The owners proved to be caring and attentive. We rested for a couple of hours, and then, as it was still midmorning, we decided to explore our new city, **Santiago de Cuba**.

We stayed in other underground locations after that. Some were great, offering tasty food, while others were dreadful and made us afraid to eat the fare they offered. We never knew what each new rental would be like until we actually arrived. Our travels through Cuba led us to many unexpected places. In all, we stayed in hotels twice, in Trinidad and Santiago de Cuba; otherwise, we stayed in our rental in Havana and the clandestine homes Jaime was able to secure for us.

FOURTEEN
SANTIAGO DE CUBA

Santiago de Cuba, Cuba's second-largest city, was founded by the Spanish in 1515. Facing the bay on the Caribbean Sea in the southeastern province of Cuba, Santiago de Cuba is known for its colonial architecture and revolutionary history. Its location may explain Haiti's and the Dominican Republic's strong influence on the Cuban culture and why both countries played such crucial roles in shaping this city's unique identity.

We visited the Castillo de San Pedro de la Roca del Morro, a UNESCO World Heritage Site since 1997. The San Pedro fort sits atop a promontory at the actual entrance to Santiago Harbor. An Italian engineer designed the fort in 1587 to protect Santiago de Cuba from pirates who were constantly attacking the city, but it was not completed until the early 1700s. By then, piracy was on the decline. The fort was eventually converted into a prison in the 1800s and then slowly fell into decline. It was restored in the 1960s, and a fort canonazo (firing of the cannon) ceremony was added for tourists. Each day as the sun sets, actors dressed in period regimentals enact the firing ceremony. The cannons blast off at the very moment the sun drops below the horizon. It is a popular tourist attraction.

We visited Santiago's most important church, the Catedral de Nuestra Senora de la Asuncion. Breathtaking with its two neoclassical towers, it was completed in 1922. The church has intricate ceiling frescoes, hand-carved choir stalls, and a polished altar entirely devoted to the Virgen de la Caridad del Cobre. This particular site has always been home to a Catholic cathedral since the city's founding.

After spending the day running around, the three of us proceeded to our latest underground home. Upon our arrival, we noted the large, rectangular yellow building looked scruffy. Moving closer to the door, we could see that large sections of the yellow paint were peeling off the building in big chunks. Shaking off our doubts, we recalled our latest host had promised food, along with beds for the night. So, with trepidation, we rang the bell.

The food was okay, so we felt slightly bad about harshly judging the building's outward appearance at first glance. After eating, we all elected to retire early. Emma and I shared a room while Jaime had been assigned a separate room in a different part of the house. Our room had two beds, a large double bed and a small twin. I offered to take the small twin, which was placed perpendicular to the larger bed. A peek into the bathroom scared us, as it was shockingly unclean. The shower water drained directly out through the hole in the middle of the floor. Adjacent to the shower was a bright cobalt-blue toilet that sat low to the ground, had no lid, and was filthy. The sink had been painted the same color to match the toilet.

I had seen enough. After splashing water onto my face to wash it, I sprinted into my nearby bed, trying not to think about our accommodations.

I am a sound sleeper; yet after a couple of hours of sleep, I awoke to the sound of hushed crying. Looking over to the bathroom, I could see Emma sitting on the edge of the grubby blue toilet, sobbing. This shocked me since it was unusual for Emma to cry. Leaping out of bed and into the bathroom a few feet away, I asked her what was wrong.

"Bedbugs kept biting me, so I couldn't sleep," Emma exclaimed in distress between hiccups, apologizing for having woke me. She confessed that, in her desperation to get some rest, she wished she knew where Jaime's room was because she would have knocked on his door and ask to sleep on the floor. There would be no more sleeping that night.

The next day, groggy from lack of sleep, Emma and I relayed our tale of woe in low whispers to Jaime over breakfast. The three of us decided to find a hotel for the next night. Thanking our hosts, we made a quick exit.

Jaime had started looking for hotels as we finished our breakfasts. He chose the San Carlos Hotel. We made our way there after breakfast because we wanted to check in early to have enough time to begin our second day's outing. We agreed to run up to our rooms, drop off our luggage, and meet back in front of the hotel in fifteen minutes. Emma and I rushed to our room, making sure to get back downstairs to meet Jaime.

When we were back downstairs, we saw no sign of Jaime outside the hotel. We looked around and waited and waited. We had no idea what had happened to him. Losing patience, we returned to the front desk and requested the desk clerk ring Jaime's room. There was no answer.

Giving up, Emma and I trudged down the stairs, planning on exiting the hotel to check if he was now out in front. As we reached the front lobby, we heard loud singing echoing from a side room, which appeared to be a bar. Our previous search hadn't included that area since it was still early morning and, well, truthfully, we never considered the bar. Upon entering the dark room, Emma and I saw Jaime standing center stage along with two musicians, singing his heart out. Smiling as he saw us enter the small bar, he continued crooning as though he did not have a care in the world. Several times, Emma and I motioned for him to come down from the stage so we could leave. He ignored us. Frustrated, we sat down, and each ordered a beer, waiting until he decided to join us. We had to admit we were surprised that Jaime had such a wonderful baritone voice.

Finally, laughing as he made his way down from the stage to our table, he said, "Let's go."

As we walked out of the hotel, Jaime casually remarked that Americans really didn't appreciate how much Cubanos loved their music. Their music was, he told us in a hushed tone, what he loved the most about Cuba.

Stepping out onto the street, we flagged down a cab. Cabs were not easily identifiable in Cuba because many citizens used their personal vehicles to provide taxi services. Some cabs were marked. Most were not. We caught an open jeep one and quickly hopped in.

Chatting among ourselves, Jaime, Emma, and I were completely engrossed in our discussion when we felt a strong jolt, then heard a loud crunching sound, followed by an even louder bang. The jeep stopped suddenly. We had crashed into a large blue 1950s sedan overflowing with people. The right side of the sedan had completely crumpled on impact.

All the passengers jumped out of the car and started running toward our jeep. It was a short distance. A young girl in a large pink ball gown led the pack, screaming at us in Spanish that we had ruined her quinceanera. In Latin cultures, a *quinceanera* is a girl's fifteenth birthday celebration. It represents her transition from childhood to adulthood and typically involves a Mass followed by a large party. It is a formal event and follows a wedding format, with maids and groomsmen and sometimes elaborate costumes. Some families save for years in order to provide their daughter with a show-stopping event. Apparently, we had interrupted the party with the crash.

The jeep suffered only minor damage, but Jaime yelled to us to get out of the jeep and run, as the situation might get dangerous. Speaking fast, he explained that most drivers in Cuba do not have car insurance, so disputes are settled in the street immediately after the crash. As we all scurried away from the jeep, Jaime stopped and turned back. He said he had to go back and help the cabdriver.

We stood a ways back and observed as two men pulled the hapless driver out of the front seat of the jeep and surrounded him. We could hear shouting but were not close enough to understand what they were saying. The uproar continued for a while and then quieted down. We could see Jaime in the middle of the group, gesturing toward the banged-up car. Suddenly, the men and the ball-gown girl set off toward the smashed-up blue sedan. The girl was still weeping as she trudged toward the car. Jaime started walking in our direction. The cabdriver climbed back into his seat and drove toward us.

Relieved the heated exchange ended without bloodshed, Emma and I asked Jaime what had gotten the people from the sedan to leave. He said he and the driver paid the group money for the damage to its car. Emma and I were afraid to ask how much money was exchanged, and we decided we would never rent a car in Cuba.

We returned to the hotel after a day of exploring Santiago de Cuba and decided to stay on to visit **Parque Baconao** the next day. Located between Santiago de Cuba and the Baconao River, it was declared a biosphere by UNESCO. Of note is the botanical garden, which is home to more than 1,800 species of flora endemic to the area.

The park was developed to showcase Cuba's history and culture. It has been expanded over time. It originally focused on the Cuban Revolution since it was built in the supposed staging area for Fidel Castro's raid on the Moncada Barracks in 1953, which led to his arrest. Many believe this site marked the beginning of the Cuban Revolution. A museum in the park is dedicated to this famous battle.

Covering eight hundred kilometers, the park includes a lagoon, several beaches for diving and fishing, and a tropical village of the pre-Columbian Caribbean people. It also sports an outdoor car museum, housing a collection of 2,500 miniature model cars. The most popular attractions, however, are the 200 life-size sculptures of roaming dinosaurs from the Jurassic period, which inmates from the local prison constructed.

Another popular site is the Great Rock (Gran Piedra), a large volcanic rock weighing more than sixty-three thousand tons. Though we visited it, we did not climb the 459 steps to the top for the panoramic view. It is said that on some nights, you can even see the lights of Jamaica from it.

Beautiful, *bizarre*, and *strange* are the words I would use to describe Parque Baconao. Its presentation of so many disparate themes made it hard to reconcile holistically. What do model cars have to do with dinosaurs? In the end, it became clear to me that its intent was to instill pride and nationalism in Cubans, and it seemed to work.

FIFTEEN
BARACOA/GUANTANAMO

Baracoa, our next destination, was three hours and seventeen minutes away. Jaime suggested we fly. In researching inexpensive flights, he managed to get us booked on a small cargo plane at a reasonable price. Emma and I were elated and secretly pleased at his fiscal astuteness. Little did we know of the adventure yet to come.

The next morning, a cab dropped us off on the runway near the plane. Emma and I were surprised by how small the plane was, but then again, we had never flown in a cargo plane before. What did we know?

Fuimos A Cuba

Our real distress began as we climbed into the plane and discovered there were no passenger seats. In fact, there were no seats at all, except ones for the pilot and the copilot. We were told the newspapers piled in high, neat stacks would serve as our individual seats for the flight. Our makeshift seats sank down as we eased into them, making a crinkly, paper-scrunching noises. Obviously, there were no seat belts.

Looking around our flimsy makeshift seats, Emma and I could see the cargo plane was packed to the brim. Every square inch was filled with cargo and more newspapers than we had ever seen in one place. We attempted to settle in, make ourselves comfortable, and not show the terror clutching at our hearts. We tried to console ourselves with the knowledge that it was only a ninety-minute flight. Seeing our panic-stricken faces, Jaime laughed and said we'd be all right. It would be a new adventure. Emma and I assuaged our anxiety by reminding ourselves we were saving money and time flying this way.

We arrived safe but rattled. We headed directly to our next underground home. On the way, Emma and I called Eduardo. We had been keeping in contact with him from time to time as a courtesy due to our unexpected and sudden departure. Not happy, he kept asking where we were and when we would be back. Patiently, we explained we were continuing our travels through Cuba and had no idea when we'd return. We were unsure why he was so upset. We were going to pay him for the apartment whether or not we were there. However, we had not spelled out the financial terms if we did not end up using the apartment, as we had never envisioned that happening, so this may have explained his unease with our extended absence. Eduardo felt he was losing money and missing the opportunity to be our travel guide.

We wanted to spend time exploring Baracoa, a municipality and city in Guantanamo Province near the eastern tip of Cuba. Baracoa is surrounded by rugged mountains on one side and the Atlantic Ocean on the other; the city's name is an Indian word meaning "beside the sea." Isolated from the rest of Cuba until the 1960s—when a road was finally built through the mountains, connecting it with Guantanamo—it is known as the place where Columbus first dropped his anchor. It holds the distinction of being the first Cuban capital.

Baracoa is a city filled with exotic foods and names that mirror its Indian past. Banana, coconut palm, and cacao are usually present on the table in some way or fashion, either in sauces, wrapped in leaves, or added to cups of chorrote, a thick local chocolate. Baracoa is known for its enchanting beaches, so we spent the day enjoying the sun and taking pictures.

Guantanamo Bay, just twenty-eight miles from Baracoa, was our next stop. **Guantanamo** (an aboriginal name that means "the land between two rivers") is a municipality and city in southwest Cuba. It is the capital of Guantanamo Province. It is served by the Caimanera Port near the site of the U.S. naval base, which shares a seventeen-mile border with Cuba.

In 1903, Cuba leased the forty-five square miles that the base sits on to the United States. This arrangement can be terminated by mutual agreement. The base has been used as a detention camp in years after our visit and was home to the famous Abu Ghraib prison. It remains a U.S. naval base today. As of May 2018, there were forty detainees at Guantanamo Bay and 5,500 personnel stationed on the base.

The city lies just fifteen kilometers away from Guantanamo Bay, a natural harbor that the United States has utilized since 1898, when it was captured from Spain. In 2004, the population was approximately 244,603; it had a slightly smaller population in the late 1990s. Sugarcane and cotton were grown in the area at the time of our visit. We spent our time shopping for gifts. We did not go onto the base, as civilians and Cubans are not allowed access. The inland city population does not mix with base personnel.

Emma and I would soon be parting ways with our traveling partner in Santiago de Cuba. Jaime was going on to South America, and we would be returning to Havana for our flight to San Francisco. Jaime agreed to find us one last underground home in Havana before taking his leave. We did not want to spend our last night in the rented apartment.

In honor of our departures, we planned a festive dinner where we exchanged addresses and laughed at the many mishaps we had experienced during our trip. Emma and I were sad to say goodbye to Jaime. He had been a faithful friend and an outstanding traveling companion. Shedding a few tears, we hugged and said our final goodbyes.

SIXTEEN
RETURNING TO HAVANA

The day after our parting dinner, Emma and I returned to Havana, going directly to our last underground home. Before knocking on the front door, Emma silently pointed to the roof, in awe. Looking up, I could see it was covered with uneven broken glass, and above the glass was a short barbwire fence that covered the entire parameter of the roof. This was clearly to discourage anyone from climbing onto it in order to enter the house. It seemed like overkill, but it would surely discourage burglaries.

After entering the house, we understood why it had a cut-glass roof. We were shocked and taken aback by the elegance, the fine furnishings, the crystal chandeliers, and the incredibly beautiful rugs throughout the house. We knew this kind of opulence had existed in an earlier era, but we thought it was now long gone. When we felt brave enough, we asked our hosts how they had acquired such exquisite things. They explained they had hidden the expensive items away for many, many years and were now finally able to bring out the more valuable items. But they told us it was still dangerous. There were lots of thieves. They had to be careful.

After showing us around their home, they took us out to their backyard to see their birds. Three beautiful parrots sat in five-foot-high cages. Each parrot had its own cage with a huge metal lock hanging on the front of the door. The cages were individually chained to a metal pole, which had been cemented to the ground. Astonished, we asked how they fed the birds. Each cage had to be unlocked daily, we were told, and the large locks were the only way to keep the parrots from being stolen.

This was our last night in Havana. We were grateful to not have to worry about bedbugs, but we did have to contend with a different sort of problem prior to leaving for home. Our luggage remained in Eduardo's apartment, and we needed to retrieve it before flying home the next morning. But we were afraid of bumping into Eduardo. Our relationship had seriously deteriorated over the course of our stay in Cuba. He had continued to worry we would renege on paying him the full amount as promised. Emma and I debated what was fair. We had been in the apartment only four out of our fourteen days in Cuba. He had been furious that we hit the road, deserting him in one fell swoop. Our reason for leaving was to escape Eduardo's persistent attention. And as it turned out, breaking free from our overzealous host was the best decision of the entire trip.

Emma and I decided to sneak into Eduardo's apartment after dark and pack quickly. We'd leave a note for Eduardo along with the money owed on the kitchen table. We did not want to run into him.

We caught a cab from our underground rental just as dusk fell. Upon arriving at our old stomping grounds, we rushed up the five flights of stairs to recover our luggage. We were happy to discover Eduardo was not there. After packing hastily, we rushed to catch a ride back to our underground home. On the way back, Emma got into an extended conversation with the cabdriver about his health and some special pills she recommended to improve it. This was her attempt to entice him to pick us up early the next morning. She was interested in helping him and hoped the promise of sending him the aforementioned pills upon our return to the Bay Area would work.

We explained we had to leave by 3:00 a.m. to catch a flight to Cancun for the connecting flight to San Francisco. Emma asked if he would be willing to pick us up. The taxi driver eagerly agreed. But something about his quick response worried me and pricked at my uneasy gut. Something told me he was just being polite and we would end up with no ride to the airport. When I shared my concerns with Emma, she shook her head and said I had no faith.

The next morning, Emma and I were ready and waiting at 3:00 a.m. Our cabdriver, as I feared, was a no-show. We had a problem. We could not miss our flight. Since we were in a quiet residential area, we walked over to the next-largest street, which was dark with limited lighting. We positioned ourselves on the corner, hoping to see cabs going in either direction. As we stood on the curb scanning the cross streets for cabs, determining which cars were taxis was difficult since so few were clearly marked. Jaime had warned us about getting into unidentified cabs.

We started trying to flag a cab down. The first one that stopped was scary, so we waved it away. We also passed on the next two. By then, we were frantic that we'd miss our flight. Finally, Emma and I agreed to get into the fourth cab, sending up a quick prayer it would be safe. We held our breath and climbed in.

The driver dropped us off at the airport, and we jumped out, running toward the check-in counter as though our lives depended on it. As we were rushing to the gate, an attendant stopped us and advised we would not be flying out on our scheduled flight. Just as the ticket agent relayed that information to us, a large contingent of Cuban families started forming a long line near us. They looked excited. We did not understand what was happening. There were lots of children and enough families to fill the plane.

We approached the ticket counter and asked why our flight was canceled and why those people were lining up to still get on our scheduled flight. We were informed that today was the "lottery flight." Frustrated after our rush to make it on time, we asked, "What the hell is a lottery flight?"

Shrugging her shoulders as though it was nothing, the ticket agent explained that every year, Cuba held a lottery for its citizens who wanted to leave Cuba for the United States. If your name was selected, you could take the flight out. It was a one-way ticket. We could not believe we had been kicked off our scheduled flight for this annual lottery. The agent said we could take the next flight; it would still allow us to make our connection. All that rushing and running for a delayed flight.

SEVENTEEN
TOO MUCH RUM

An hour later, as we boarded another plane, we grasped our other problem, which had slipped our minds. The flight mix-up had so distracted us that we had forgotten we had too many bottles of rum in our carry-on bags. We had four bottles of exceptionally good Cuban rum we could not take back to the United States. We had not had time to drink from any of the bottles since purchasing them at the rum factory. We had to do something. So we decided to drink them all. We asked the airline stewardess for cups, careful to keep our rum bottles out of sight.

Things were going well. We had almost finished one bottle of our delectable rum when it slipped out of our hands as the plane hit a bumpy air pocket. The bottle quickly rolled under the seat in front of us, and before we could grab it, it bounced out into the main aisle. It then started rolling toward the front of the plane.

Stunned and fearful, we had no idea what to do. We hoped no one would notice, but it was making a lot of noise as it rolled back and forth with every lurch of the plane. The man in front of us turned around and stared at us. By now, we were feeling no pain, so we returned his stare with smiles. What else could we do? The stewardess rushed down the aisle and picked up the bottle, trying to see where it came from. We kept our heads down, hoping not to be identified as the culprits.

I hissed to Emma, "How are we going to finish the remaining three bottles before we get to San Francisco?"

Nodding knowingly, she reminded me we had some layover time in Cancun. We could drink them there, she said, hoping to calm me. Emma is not a good drinker, so I was really distraught. We would have to dispose of the leftover bottles in Cancun.

We were feeling surprisingly good by the time we reached Cancun. We had a couple of hours before our flight to San Francisco, so we decided to finish off our remaining bottles at a corner table in an airport bar; that seemed to be the best place, but we would have to be discreet. Keeping an eye on the bartender, we noticed he was giving out limes with all the drink orders. Emma and I needed limes if we were going to get through the last three bottles of rum. How could we drink rum without limes?

We had an idea. Smiling and holding our bottle up so people could see the label, we walked around, offering a quick pour for a couple of limes and making sure the bartender didn't see what we were up to. We felt sharing was the best way to go because we could not drink all the rum anyway. Some patrons were startled by our offer as we poured generously. Most were happy to oblige us, and some even handed over the limes while declining the rum. Others just declined, thinking it strange that two women were handing out free drinks in a bar.

Our sharing plan enabled us to finish our second bottle and open up our third bottle. We decided to leave the last full bottle on the back table of the bar and finish the third one on the plane, but we would have to be more careful. We were not willing to risk repeating the earlier plane scenario.

EIGHTEEN
HIDING THE CIGARS

With our rum problem partially resolved, we moved on to solving our next dilemma. We had bought too many cigars as gifts and needed to hide them before boarding our final flight. Luckily, we had come prepared for this particular task. We were going to duct-tape the cigars onto our bodies so they would not be visible once we were completely dressed. We had always planned to do this in a restroom during the Cancun layover but had gotten so distracted with finishing up the rum that we were running late.

Although we had thought ourselves so clever, we soon discovered this was not going to work. After taping a couple of cigars to our bodies, we realized the fat and bulky cigars would cause visible bulges in our clothing. Pausing our taping, we ran out to the airport gift shop to buy extra-large blouses that would hopefully hide our contraband. Once we had our new tops in hand, we headed back to the ladies' room, locking the door before recommencing our taping.

Every so often, there would be repeated banging on the door. Shouting out in Spanish that the restroom was out of order worked for a while, as it discouraged patrons who wanted access to the restroom. It succeeded until an airport attendant came by with a key and unlocked the door. We were just able to pull our tops down over the contraband cigars as she entered, but she caught a glimpse of the silver duct tape. Her face made it clear she thought we were taping drugs onto ourselves.

When she asked why we had locked the door, we made a flimsy excuse about being sick. Frowning, the attendant told us we had to leave as she pointedly held the door open for us to exit. We had almost finished our taping before she entered, so with guilty expressions, we slunk out of the restroom, searching for another bathroom to finish the job. When we were done, we looked like fat Americans but not like the smugglers we really were.

If someone had manually searched us on our return flight to San Francisco, we would have been caught; but in those years, body scanning was not fully utilized. So, with our oversize tops, we hoped to smuggle all our cigars into the United States.

With all the rushing about and duct-taping, I somehow misplaced my return ticket. Emma and I searched everything but could not find it. We knew we had to go back to the earlier bathroom to see if it was in the trash can. Worried that the attendant might still be around, we approached carefully, but she had left. We turned the trash can upside down and started meticulously sorting through the mess of papers and miscellaneous garbage. It was a messy job. But we found the ticket. It had been torn in half, and it had duct tape stuck on it. How this had happened we could not fathom. More important, we were not sure whether the torn ticket would be accepted, even though it had not yet been used.

I headed back to the check-in desk with my torn ticket; there, the agent told me I would have to pay for a new one. I was so relieved to have a ticket that I simply handed her the additional cash payment.

We sat down and waited for our flight to be called. It had been an exhausting day with the 3:00 a.m. cab ride, all the drinking on the plane and at the Cancun airport, the cigar taping, and the trash can searching to find my lost ticket. Thank goodness we found it. I no longer cared that I had to pay an additional fee to get a new ticket. I was going home.

NINETEEN

HOME AT LAST

After boarding our final flight and settling in, we pulled out the remaining bottle of rum. Staring at the golden liquid, we tried to convince ourselves we could drink a little more. We had imbibed a lot of rum already, so we were not sure how much more we could force down. Taking a deep breath, we unscrewed the cap and each took a couple of sips. Yes, we both agreed it was delicious, but we were done with the rum. Neither of us could sip another drop.

We were oh so tired and worried that we might have trouble getting through customs in San Francisco. We had drunk too much rum and were sweating from all the duct tape stuck on us to hold the cigars in place. It had been a long trip, and we did not want it to end badly as we crossed back into the United States. We crossed our fingers, put the cap on the rum, and placed the bottle in the seat pouch in front of us.

Soon thereafter, the pilot announced our approach to the San Francisco airport. We were so happy to be back in the United States. Just before exiting the plane, we covered the remaining bottle in the front pouch with newspapers to disguise it as best we could and left it on the plane for some lucky person.

Standing in the customs line, we prayed we would get through it without being searched. We were hot and sticky from all the duct tape and anxious to get it and the cigars off our bodies. In the end, there was no need for prayers. We were quickly whisked through the line. Three international flights had arrived at the same time, and airport staff were anxious to move everyone through customs efficiently and without delay.

Outside the airport, Emma and I hugged. We both wanted to kiss the ground but restrained ourselves, exhaling huge sighs of relief instead. We had made it home safely after all that had happened. We were ecstatic to be standing on U.S soil once again. Our only regret was we didn't have those bottles of rum to savor and help us recall our Cuban adventures.

CPSIA information can be obtained
at www.ICGtesting.com
Printed in the USA
LVHW041507111120
671410LV00027B/173